The Trip

Written by Leya Roberts
Illustrated by Andy San Diego

"Ho hum," said Giraffe.

"Yes, ho hum," said Zebra.

3

"Let's take a trip," said Giraffe.

"Yes, let's take a trip," said Zebra.

4

Giraffe and Zebra ran across the grass.

Giraffe and Zebra ran across the rocks.

Giraffe and Zebra ran across the hills.

Giraffe and Zebra ran across the river.

Giraffe and Zebra ran across Lion's den.

"Yikes!" said Giraffe.

"Yikes!" said Zebra.

10

"ROAR!" said Lion.

Giraffe and Zebra zoomed across the river.

Giraffe and Zebra zoomed across the hills.

Giraffe and Zebra zoomed across the rocks.

Giraffe and Zebra zoomed across the grass.

"I love it here," said Giraffe.

"Yes, I love it here, too!" said Zebra.